Playtime Rhymes

Compiled by John Foster
Illustrated by Carol Thompson

Oxford University Press
Oxford   New York   Toronto

Oxford University Press, Great Clarendon Street, Oxford OX2 6DP

Oxford   New York
Athens Auckland Bangkok Bogota Bombay
Buenos Aires Calcutta Cape Town Dar es Salaam
Delhi Florence Hong Kong Istanbul Karachi
Kuala Lumpur Madras Madrid Melbourne
Mexico City Nairobi Paris Singapore
Taipei Tokyo Toronto Warsaw

and associated companies in
Berlin   Ibadan

Oxford is a trade mark of Oxford University Press

This selection and arrangement © John Foster 1998
Illustrations © Carol Thompson 1998
First published 1998

John Foster and Carol Thompson have asserted their moral
right to be identified as the authors of this work.

A CIP catalogue record for this book is available
from the British Library

ISBN 0 19 276163 3 (paperback)
ISBN 0 19 276206 0 (hardback)

Printed in Belgium

Contents

Ball Games

One, two, three, four.
Bounce the ball upon the floor.

Five, six, seven, eight.
Kick the ball and kick it straight.

Nine, ten,
Nine, ten.
Someone kick it back again.

Marian Swinger

1 · 2 · 3 · 4 · 5

The Ball Song

Throw me up and catch me,
bounce me on the ground,
put me down and twist me,
twizzle me around.

Drop me on the floor,
kick me at the wall.
Bounce me! Bounce me!
I'm a bouncy ball.

Tony Mitton

6 · 7 · 8 · 9 · 10

POP!

What the Bubble Said

You can't catch me!
said the bubble.
See that tree?
I can fly to the top!

Oh no you can't,
said the blackbird.
See this beak?
I can make you

POP!

Judith Nicholls

Hush-a-Bye Dragon

Hush-a-bye Dragon
on a kite-tail,
when the wind blows
the dragon will sail.

When the wind stops,
the kite-tail will swoop,
down will come Dragon
looping-the-loop.

Moira Andrew

Playdough People

Playdough people
are floppy and fat.
Some wear a funny old
playdough hat.

Playdough people
have playdough faces,
with blobs for noses
and hair like laces.

Playdough people
have bendy legs,
ears like pancakes,
eyes like eggs.

Playdough people
roll up in a ball.
Then playdough people
aren't people at all.

Tony Mitton

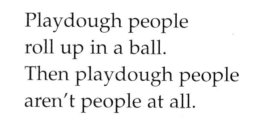

My Colouring Book

There's a letter-box
In my colouring book.
I've coloured it red.
Come and look.

There's a little chick
In my colouring book.
I've coloured it yellow.
Come and look.

There's a Christmas tree
In my colouring book.
I've coloured it green.
Come and look.

There's a big fat cat
In my colouring book.
I've coloured it purple.
Come and look.

Trevor Millum

15

Bouncing Round the Playground

Bouncing round the playground
Like a kangaroo;
We're going to Australia,
You can come too.

Waddling round the playground
Like the penguins do;
We're going to the South Pole,
You can come too.

Whizzing round the playground
Like a rocket ship;
We're going to the Milky Way . . .
Have a good trip.

Mike Jubb

17

Hunting For Treasure

This is my treasure map.
This is my boat.
These are the waves
where I rock and float.

There is the island
I'm headed for.
This is the way
that I wade ashore.

This is the spot.
This is my spade.
This is the deep,
dark hole I made.

This is the box
that I dug from the ground.
And these are the golden
coins I found.

Tony Mitton

You Can't Catch Me!

I chased Tina.
Tina chased Lee.
Lee chased Pat.
Pat chased me.

In and out the bushes.
Round and round the tree.
Up and down the path.
You can't catch me!

I chased Pat.
Pat chased Lee.
Lee chased Tina.
Tina chased me.

John Foster

The Playtime Puddle Rhyme

Puddle, splash, puddle, splash,
Don't go near the puddle, splash.
You'll get into trouble, splash,
So don't go near the puddle—SPLASH!

Mike Jubb

21

Skipping Rope Spell

Turn rope turn
don't trip my feet.
Turn rope turn
for my skipping feet.

Turn rope turn
turn round and round.
Turn in the air
turn on the ground.

One for your high
one for your low.
Turn rope turn
not too fast, not too slow.

Turn rope turn
turn to the north
turn to the south.
But please, rope, please,
don't make me out.

John Agard

Copycat

Copy everything I do.
Me first, then you.

Hold your hands up.
Scratch your head.

Point to something
that is red.

Jump about.
Then be a tree.

Be a teapot
full of tea.

Be a balloon
about to burst.
All right—now
you go first.

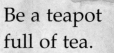

Jill Townsend

Boo!

Hop on one foot,
Jump on two,
Turn right round
And shout out
Boo!

Jennifer Tweedie

25

One Last Go

I know it's time to go now.
I know it's time, I know.
But please, Dad; please, Dad,
Can I have one last go?

One more go on the see-saw.
One more go on the swing.
One more go on the roundabout.
One more on everything.

One more go on the climbing-frame.
One more go on the slide.
One more go on the motor-bike.
One last ride!

Tony Mitton

Last One Back

Stand on one leg
Touch your nose
Jump for the sky
And land on your toes
Run for the climbing frame
Run for the tree
The last one back
Is a chimpanzee

Roger Stevens

We are grateful to the following for permission to publish their poems for the first time in this collection:

Moira Andrew: 'Hush-a-bye Dragon', Copyright © Moira Andrew 1998. **John Foster:** 'You Can't Catch Me', Copyright © John Foster 1998. **Mike Jubb:** 'The Playtime Puddle Rhyme' and 'Bouncing Round the Playground', both Copyright © Mike Jubb 1998. **Trevor Millum:** 'My Colouring Book', Copyright © Trevor Millum 1998. **Tony Mitton:** 'The Ball Song', 'Playdough People', 'Hunting for Treasure', and 'One Last Go', all Copyright © Tony Mitton 1998. **Judith Nicholls:** 'What the Bubble Said', Copyright © Judith Nicholls 1998. **Roger Stevens:** 'Last One Back', Copyright © Roger Stevens 1998. **Marian Swinger:** 'Ball Games', Copyright © Marian Swinger 1998. **Jill Townsend:** 'Copycat', Copyright © Jill Townsend 1998. **Jennifer Tweedie:** 'Boo!', Copyright © Jennifer Tweedie 1998.

We also acknowledge permission to include previously published poems:

John Agard: 'Skipping Rope Spell' from *No Hickory No Dickory No Dock* by John Agard and Grace Nichols (Viking, 1991), Copyright © John Agard 1991, reprinted by permission of the author c/o Caroline Sheldon Literary Agency.